# Jessie J

## KEEPING IT REAL

Publisher and Creative Director: Nick Wells
Project Editor: Polly Prior
Picture Research: Laura Bulbeck
Art Director and Layout Design: Mike Spender
Digital Design and Production: Chris Herbert

Special thanks to: Stephen Feather, Dawn Laker & Daniela Nava

**FLAME TREE PUBLISHING**
Crabtree Hall, Crabtree Lane
Fulham, London SW6 6TY
United Kingdom

www.flametreepublishing.com

First published 2012

12 14 16 15 13
1 3 5 7 9 10 8 6 4 2

A CIP record for this book is available from the British Library upon request.

ISBN 978-0-85775-560-5
Printed in China

# Jessie J

## KEEPING IT REAL

ALICE HUDSON

FOREWORD: MANGO SAUL, EDITOR OF SUGARSCAPE.COM

**FLAME TREE
PUBLISHING**

# Contents

# Foreword

**I first met Jessie J after she became a household name.** It was on the red carpet of a music event and to be honest I feared the worst: like many celebrities I meet after colossal success, I find they transform into prima donnas. And that's not just the women!

As Jessica Ellen Cornish approached the media scrum, the only thing that was noticeable was her conspicuously unconventional outfit, huge grin and eyes like an excited kid looking for fun. There wasn't a diva in sight and meeting her again a few months later, even after a No. 1 record, she remained the same Jessie J. Not only is she normal, she's humble, kind and beautiful too. The singer from Chadwell Heath in London really is the whole package; and with her musical talent too, Jessie J is going to be on a whole lot of playlists.

Whenever you meet Jessie J, you notice she's a fighter. Read this book and you'll discover she's been through some pretty harsh lows but always comes out on top. And to be a nice person after all she's been through is a credit to her. But the quality I admire the most about Jessie J is that she works her socks off. Having wanted to sing since she was a child, Jessie knew that nothing could stop her dream. An ideal role model for anyone wanting to go into the music business, her advice would probably be: Stay focused, work hard and be nice! Three pillars that have got Jessie J where she is today.

**Mango Saul**

Editor, sugarscape.com

# All About The Success

**Jessie J's rise** from relative anonymity to international pop star status appeared meteoric – even by showbiz standards. Before the November 2010 release of catchy, attitudinal urban hit 'Do It Like A Dude', the average music fan had never heard of her.

Yet Jessie had spent nearly four of the previous six years as a signed artist. She had written hundreds of her own songs and – having co-written tunes for the likes of Alicia Keys and Miley Cyrus – had a good reputation as a 'songwriter to the stars'. By the beginning of 2010, with no album to her name, the then-22 year old had begun to doubt she would ever really 'make it' as a solo artist, even though her dream had always been a performance and recording career of her own.

## Climbing The Charts

When her time eventually came, Jessie was more than ready. She did not so much step as storm into the spotlight. She has taken home a series of high-profile industry awards, including a BRIT and four MOBOs, and six of her singles have since charted in the UK Top 10, two of them becoming No. 1s. UK album sales have seen debut album *Who You Are* (2011) certified double platinum. After an initially lukewarm response, Jessie's smash hit 'Domino' was the track that finally earned her serious US airtime, reaching No. 6 on the *Billboard* chart. In 2012, her star has risen still further as a mentor on BBC's *The Voice UK*.

'If any singer has the potential to be the British Katy Perry or Pink, with the accompanying millions of sales, it's her. [ Her songs] are delivered with a confidence that money can't buy.'
Caroline Sullivan, in The Guardian

## Music For All Tastes

By March 2012, the official 'Do It Like A Dude' music video had been viewed over 19 million times on YouTube. Yet Jessie feels she is just getting started. Her unconventional genre-crossing style (mainly R&B, pop and hip hop) is paired with a powerful voice that is pure soul. 'It's like my album is an iPod,' she has said of *Who You Are*. 'It's like when you go clubbing these days you don't have a pop room and a separate R&B room; they're all together. People just appreciate great music.'

'I'm very open and it's funny because people say I'm very mysterious. They want me to be mysterious. I don't think I am at all. I think they want me to be mysterious because that's what they're used to.'

Jessie J

With a desire to inspire, Jessie believes she is 'not just an artist but a therapist' too. The meaning of the 'J' that she has adopted as a last name remains something of a mystery. She has told various journalists that it stands for 'Jazzhands' (a reference to her BRIT School days) and 'Jetlag' (from being a frequent flier), as well as 'for whatever you want it to'.

## Confident Woman

Jessie J oozes confidence. Refreshingly honest and outspoken, she is unafraid to be openly proud of her achievements – or to strive for greater ones. As noted by *MTV Push*, the 'singer, songwriter and show pony' has the enviable ability to excel all round. A 1.75 m (5 ft 9 in) lithe bombshell, known for her trademark razor-sharp raven fringe, Jessie is edgy and cool, talented and intelligent – and *extremely* media savvy.

She is not afraid to be different either. Jessie is open about her bisexuality and does not care what people think; she seems to have the tough skin required to succeed in the music industry. 'You know, I always say: how would you fall in love if everybody looked the same?' she has commented. 'How would music be judged if we all sounded the same? To some people I have the best voice in the world; to others I sound like a dying dolphin, so it's just taste.' Jessie is now widely looked upon as a role model and inspiration to her growing legions of young fans.

# Who's Laughing Now?

**Jessie's rise from obscurity** to household name may have seemed to happen almost overnight, but the truth is that the Essex lass had been grafting hard for many years, refusing to give up despite having come across various obstacles on her journey to make her voice heard. The young artist's success can be attributed in part to her obvious talent as a performer and songwriter, but also to her inherent determination and ability to stay focused.

'For all those people who were horrible to me, I now say: "Who's laughing now?"

Jessie J

## Music Is The Best Medicine

Possessing a vibrant persona, the energetic Jessie practically bubbles with positive energy and enthusiasm for life, both on stage and in interviews. Many of her songs feature inspirational lyrics about achieving dreams, so it is difficult to imagine the star feeling down or uninspired. Yet the singer

'People sometimes ask me "who styled you? Who wrote your songs?" I'm like, "I did! I've got a personality." That's why I started writing music in the first place.'

Jessie J

told the media that she was unhappy for seven whole years prior to the release of first album *Who You Are*. 'I was in a bad place and I was scared that I couldn't get out of it,' she confessed. Dealing firstly with school bullies and significant health problems, and then with a series of career knock-backs, in times of trouble Jessie always had music to turn to. 'It isn't a cure; it's a healer,' she has said. In particular, she found solace from trouble in songwriting, and often defied her dark moods by writing uplifting lyrics and melodies. 'I wrote such upbeat music as a way of trying to escape how I felt.'

*'When I'm in the studio sometimes,
I think no, I don't need a therapist.
I just need to write a great song.'
Jessie J*

## More Than A Voice

Naturally, multi-talented as a singer, songwriter, dancer, television personality and all-round show pony, Jessie is not one to balk at the idea of branching out, work-wise. In March 2011, she announced she was in talks with theatre bosses to bring a budding idea for an 'inspirational musical'

'Being on stage is my home. Even if it's twenty minutes, I'll take control of it because that is my time. It's when I come to life. It's just me, my heels and my mic.'

Jessie J

to life and she told the *News of the World*, 'I want to take what my album's done and take that spirit on stage. It's about teaming my love of music with my love of musical theatre.' However, plans were put on hold in 2012 due to her busy schedule. In March 2012, it was announced that the singer would be releasing her memoirs later that year. She has also stamped her clean-living, yet funky, ghetto glam image to products such as glacéau vitaminwater™, for which she is the official Olympic Ambassador.

## Healthy Matters

At age 11, Jessie was diagnosed with an irregular heartbeat. 'I had wires put in my shoulder, groin and heart to try and zap it to a normal rhythm but it didn't really work,' she recalls. At 18, Jessie suffered a minor stroke along with further heart problems. 'It was scary but I'm fine now.' The shock made her realize that nothing in life can be taken for granted. From that moment on, she became convinced that looking after her body was of upmost concern. And so was achieving her goals. 'I've looked the big stuff straight in the eye,' she told *MTV Push*. 'I've had people sitting on the end of a hospital bed, wondering what's going to happen next and genuinely not knowing. I don't drink. I don't smoke. I can't take drugs. I can't even have caffeine.'

Her health issues have helped to make her stronger and recognize the importance of following dreams and realising ambitions. 'I have to be confident. Because I can't intoxicate myself with those props ordinary young people have to give them confidence,' she says.

*'To even have someone like her to take time out of her busy schedule to know someone like me is just an honour. I love you too, Nicki.'*

*Jessie J, showing her humble side in response to praise from Nicki Minaj*

## Sounds Like?

**Jessie J is known for her catchy**, sassy tunes ('Do It Like A Dude') and powerful, soulful voice ('Domino'). Her music can loosely be described as urban pop but is laced with generous helpings of contemporary R&B as well as funk and hip hop overtones. Music-obsessed her whole life, Jessie cites a wide range of early influences and says they helped to mould her into the musician she is today. As a young girl, her tastes were shaped by sounds from her parents' CD player. Singers she was exposed to include artists who Jessie has called 'the greats': Aretha Franklin, Michael Jackson and Prince. Soul funk bands were also popular in her household. 'My dad was a huge funk fan so, you know, Funkadelic, D Train, The Gap Band... I'm lucky [my parents] had good taste in music because I wouldn't be talking to you if they hadn't,' Jessie joked with one interviewer.

## Jessie's Idols

As she entered her teens, sights now firmly set on making music a career, Jessie was also heavily influenced and inspired by popular artists of her generation, especially the group TLC. However, she told *The Independent* that if she were ever forced to pick a music idol, it would be a tough choice between Whitney Houston and Mariah Carey. Her admiration for the legendary female vocalists may explain Jessie's love of melisma – a singer's term for the use of several notes on one song syllable and a technique popular with both Carey and the late Houston. Who would have

'I mean, the best thing about growing up in a family that loves music is that you get everything from TLC to The Beatles to Michael Jackson to Tracy Chapman, you know, music is beautiful because it doesn't all sound the same...'

Jessie J

thought that the girl who grew up belting out Houston tracks holding a hairbrush in front of her mirror would go on to perform an emotional version of her own song – the title track from the album *Who You Are* – in tribute (at a pre-Grammy event), following Houston's tragic death?

'She's literally made normal artists and music boring, which bothers me. It annoys me when people say Leona Lewis is boring. No, she's not. She's got a sick voice and being normal is cool.'

Jessie J on the Lady Gaga effect

## Currently Speaking

Jessie J told *Singersroom* in March 2011 that she was 'addicted' to Jazmine Sullivan and Kim Burrell, and that she was also 'a huge fan' of Nicki Minaj. For the latter, the feeling is mutual, with Minaj telling *MTV News* in February 2011 that she was 'in love' with Jessie, to which Jessie later responded, 'What can you say when someone like Nicki Minaj says that they're in love with you? I am obsessed with her; I think that she is a

superstar.' Other current artists she likes include Beyoncé, whom Jessie admires for her consistency, and Rihanna, who is one of her 'style icons' and about whom she gushed to MTV, 'She's a pop star; she oozes it. She's everything I want to be!' She also admires rappers Lil Wayne and Drake.

'I am so, like, the *uncoolest person ever. My dad's cooler than me. He was the one playing D Train and Funkadelic in the house. I will not lie.'* Jessie J

## Jessie Likes...

When asked in 2011 by NME.com to write about her favourite album from the past 15 years, she named Lauryn Hill's debut solo effort *The Miseducation of Lauryn Hill* (1998). 'I have a really clear memory of listening to it while walking to school, aged 12,' Jessie wrote. 'I loved songs like "Everything Is Everything" and "Ex-Factor".' The emotional, soulful style of the album's tracklist inspired Jessie to become a songwriter more than any other. She recalls listening to the CD time and time again, thinking, 'This is what I want to do with my life. I want to write songs like that, songs that everyone can relate to.'

# Who Are You?

**Jessica Ellen Cornish** was born in Chadwell Heath, in the Greater London Borough of Redbridge, Essex, on 27 March 1988. She is the youngest of three girls. Her father Stephen is a social worker and her mother Rose is a nursery teacher. Jessie is extremely close to her parents, who provided the youngster with a supportive environment and taught her the importance of kindness and charity from a young age.

'The first song I ever wrote I was nine. I don't really talk about it much because it's pretty bad. It was like: "There is never freedom, in a world like ours. People always dying, what is it all about?" And I was nine! Seriously intense child.'

Jessie J

'Give me something to draw or an outfit to pick for someone, or hair, make-up, acting, write a song, I'm fine with it, but anything to do with sums – it was never my thing.'

Jessie J

## Family Ties

Jessie has said she believes it was her father's influence which led to many of her songs having a 'therapeutic' edge. 'The advice he has given me has really influenced how I write my songs,' she noted in a video interview posted on the Jessie J Online website. She has said that while the entire family are 'performers' in a way – 'All of us are like comedians … like at Christmas it's about who can get the most laughs' – she was the only one who wanted to sing and write songs. Big sister Hannah is a former drama teacher now turned photographer, while her other sibling Rachel is a creative writer who has worked as a learning mentor and child minder.

## Young Talent

Unlike her academic sisters, both former 'head girls', Jessie claims she missed out on the clever gene and was 'never really that good at anything' as far as her schoolwork was concerned. 'At school they were like. "Oh, you're a Cornish girl" and they kind of expected me to be the same as my sisters,' she told *The Independent*. However, Jessie was never one to measure success by exam results. Music was always her 'thing'; her first words as a baby were 'jam hot': lyrics from the 1990 hit 'Dub Be Good To Me'. Her first ambition in life was to star in musical theatre and she attended Colin's Performing Arts School. Jessie has admitted that she was 'a little show-off' as a child. 'I was always very bubbly, always thought I was the funny one, and was a bit of

a tomboy.' Jessie was constantly singing in front of the mirror, hairbrush mic in hand. She and her elder sisters even formed a 'band', cheesily called 'The Three Cornish Pasties', with Hannah on piano, Rachel on trombone and, of course, Jessie as the vocalist.

## Bullied!

Despite her bubbly personality or, more likely, because of it, Jessie was bullied at school. 'It was in a malicious, horrible way,' she recounted. 'Kids used to throw stones at my head.' Poor Jessie was even banned from the school choir for singing too loudly. 'I was in it for a day and some of the adults were moaning that their kids were upset I was too good. I was eleven. Can you imagine? I was heartbroken.'

While this was clearly a nasty experience, Jessie is adamant that being bullied only made her stronger – something she would later draw upon musically, explicitly in the funky track 'Who's Laughing Now' in which she sings: 'Thank you for the pain; it made me raise my game.' With the song's video featuring a mini Jessie getting picked on at school, the track also points out how ironic it is that these people are trying to jump on the wagon now she's successful: 'Oh Jessie, I saw you on YouTube. I tagged old photos from when we was at school.' In the track, Jessie tells them to remember how they 'dragged my spirit down'.

'My family is very creative, but no one in my family sings ... I was the only one who put my life to a melody.'

Jessie J

## It All Starts Here

**Jessie was just 11 years old** when she auditioned for, and won, a part as Brat in Andrew Lloyd Webber's production of *Whistle Down The Wind*. Her first gig lasted a full two years. 'That was when it all started,' she recalls, adding that the cast used to call her 'Brat Pit' due to an incident one night when she fell off the stage and into the orchestra pit. 'I think Andrew Lloyd Webber thought I was going to sue him. He really cosied up after that.' Jessie relished this early opportunity to indulge her passion in a professional capacity. 'You can get paid for this?' she recalls thinking at the time: 'Bring it on.' She began taking dance classes at the weekends and, at the age of 16, the director of *Evita* invited her to audition. She did not get the part but, according to Jessie, only because she was 'too young'.

## A Brit Thing

Her focus still firmly set on a career in musical theatre, Jessie was accepted at the age of 16 into the BRIT School for Performing Arts and Technology in Croydon, just south of London. She began studying musical theatre, before her true calling as a singer-songwriter emerged. 'I didn't really want to be an artist; I kind of spent my whole life training to be on the stage.' Whilst at the famous school, Jessie ended up auditioning for a girl band, solely 'because everybody

'When someone slams a door in my face, I try to find a bigger key or a chisel to try to break it down. I knew that wasn't the end of me; it was the beginning.'

Jessie J

> 'I'm doing *Saturday Night Live* on *TV*, which she did *early* on too. I don't *drink* but when we meet I'll have a *Lucozade* and *Adele* will have a *pint*. It'll be a *right giggle*.'
>
> *Jessie J*

else was'. She got in and stayed with the group called Soul Deep for two years. 'I knew it was a way for me to kind of be able to get better without being in the limelight. It was kind of like a development deal, being in a girl band.'

## Famous Friends

However, she also said that being in a group knocked her confidence as a songwriter. 'Obviously, when you're in a girl band, no one writes their own songs – do you know what I mean?' She left due to her belief that 'it wasn't going anywhere'. Jessie graduated from the BRIT School alongside fellow famous singers Adele and Leona Lewis in 2006. 'I used to have jamming sessions with Adele between classes. I am so proud of how well she's doing. She is amazing. When we met up with each other it was like "babe" this and "babe" that.'

## Dud Deal

Jessie was signed to independent London-based label Gut Records – Tom Jones's former label. Jessie has said she wrote between 100 and 150 songs over a two-year period but then, just as she was about to release her first single, the label went bust. 'Someone told me on the telephone. They've gone into liquidation. I didn't even know what it meant. Liquidization? What, they've been turned

into a soup?' She tried hard not to let the set-back get her down and, with typical determination, started shopping herself around the UK labels, but none were interested in signing her. 'They said they didn't get it and didn't think they could work with me. A lot of girls were about to dominate the industry at the time. I felt I missed my chance.' Jessie was disillusioned, yet refused to quit and *never* considered giving up songwriting.

'*I think it was **that** that made me **grow up** really **fast** because I was going through **school** to do a **show every night**. It made me **realize** that I could do **what** I love and be **paid** for it.*'

Jessie, on being cast in the West End aged 11

toured with Macy Gray, The Sugababes, Girls Aloud and Chris Brown. Her songwriting gained momentum and earned attention from artists including Brown, Lisa Lois – the winner of Holland's *X Factor* – Alicia Keys, Justin Timberlake and Christina Aguilera.

*'I'm glad I had to learn how to be amazing on stage like that: how to fill somewhere the size of Wembley Arena with no press, no features, no record, no band behind me. It toughens you up.'*

Jessie J

## Party On

It was the track 'Party In The U.S.A.', co-written with Dr. Luke and Claude Kelly, that would finally give Jessie her first taste of high-ranking, but unsung, achievement. In 2009 the track reached the Top 10 of charts in eight countries. 'You can't really ask for much more, to be honest,' Jessie said. 'I

recorded "Party In The U.S.A.", played it for the label but they didn't think it was right for me. So they pitched it and two weeks later it was No. 1 in six countries [sung by Miley Cyrus].' Dr. Luke texted her to let her know about the song's huge success and Jessie at first 'didn't believe him'. She thinks the song is better suited to Miley than herself: 'It's way too straight pop for me. The version I wrote and demoed on that day was well ironic.'

## Lost In La-La Land

The song 'Who You Are', which eventually became the album title track, was written the same week as 'Party In The U.S.A.', yet the former – a soulful number – could not be more different. She was in LA feeling homesick, lost and fed up, and 'trying to remember who I was' whilst being 'surrounded by all these women who looked so Hollywood perfect on the outside,' she recalls. 'The most important thing in life is to be happy, but everything had become too "business" and sterile.' That day, when she walked into the studio, Jessie said she did not even want to be there. 'I would've rather been in Essex, eating pie and mash and watching an old episode of *One Foot in the Grave*. The words just fell out of me. It was exactly what I wanted to say about myself when I was that lost.'

Advice given to her by Justin Timberlake, who publicly deemed her 'the best singer in the world right now', helped to ground her. 'He said, "Make sure you play this to win. Don't do it for the fame or success; do it because you love it and want to make a change' – and that's how I've always lived my career.'

'Everything had become too business-like and sterile. I really thought I was going to quit – not music, but the music industry. I was really down, but when I'm down, I write a song about it.'

Jessie J, on writing the track 'Who You Are'

# In Her Own Right

'**Get yourself out there as much** as you can and film everything' is Jessie's advice for budding artists. Combined with her songwriting credits, Jessie's obsession with filming 'everything' is what led to her big break. Record executives, such as Jason Flom at Lava, were sent links to her Myspace page. Represented by her agency at the time, William Morris, in 2008 she jetted back to the US, where she performed a showcase at the Viper Rooms and, according to the singer herself, two days later had eight offers. 'LA [Reid] said to me he couldn't believe that British labels had passed up on me,' the singer told an interviewer with typical confidence. A bidding war kicked off; initially, Jessie was not allowed to speak with labels directly, but after several months of negotiations – and a change of management for Jessie – a deal was eventually signed in late 2008 with Lava/Universal Republic. Meanwhile, back in the UK, 'Everyone suddenly loved the idea of signing me. I got to choose and went to Island Records. I'm so thankful.'

## 'Do It Like A Dude'

When Jessie first wrote catchy urban track 'Do It Like A Dude', she envisaged it on Rihanna's set list – Jessie reckons it was partly inspired by Rihanna's 'Rude Boy'. Yet, after she sent the tune to Island, the label insisted Jessie hang on to the track for herself. It was the single they had been waiting for.

'I never had a band. It was me, my CD, my heels and a huge stage to fill. I loved that I had no one and nothing to hide behind.'

Jessie J

Almost two years after signing, she finally had her first release via download in November 2010 (and as a physical release in January 2011). The track reached the No. 2 spot in the UK. Brash and bolshy, some interpreted it as overtly sexual, while others reckoned it was about hating men – Jessie herself freely admits, 'I wanted to shake up some controversy and I definitely think that record did that.' She said the song was born when she started freestyling 'like a dude' in the studio one day in parody of a producer who wore 'ridiculously low' jeans. 'I wanted to write a song that was tongue-in-cheek and a parody of a stereotypical male. But also, I wanted the song to be empowering for girls, but not kind of an "I hate men" song – because I don't and I don't say that in the song. It's about feeling hardcore.'

## Video Star

Finally, Jessie was able to begin to enjoy the career experiences she had longed for, such as making her first music video. Directed by Emil Nava, the provocative video for 'Do It Like A Dude' was shot in the basement of a church. It features Jessie and a team of female back-up dancers, many dressed like 'dudes', giving attitude to one another, smoking and drinking. Jessie wears one of her – now trademark – bodycon leotards. 'It's a bit weird; I feel a bit wrong, you know, dressed like this in the bottom of a church but um, yeah I'll do some good deeds tomorrow,' she jokes on tape at the shoot – being Jessie, of course, she had the experience filmed.

## Shocking Scenes

Director Nava has described the concept for the video as 'Like an underground apocalyptic world with girls – sort of like *Mad Max* meets warriors meets *Blade Runner*; that sort of attitude.' He said of Jessie, 'She's great. She's just great; she's very easy to film. She's photogenic, and exciting and fresh.'

Meanwhile, Jessie has said of the video: 'I wanted it to be what it is. I concepted it as ghetto chic. Girls grabbing their "dicks"? What's wrong with that? It's "gully". But it's pop enough to go both ways.' She admitted that the 'epic' filming experience 'felt like my wedding day' and was very emotional. And then it was over: 'All that build-up and it was over in nineteen hours.'

'Within two days of the showcases in New York and LA, I found myself sitting with the head of every label in the US. There I was, sitting with Clive Davis, who signed Whitney Houston and Janis Joplin.'

Jessie J

# 'Price Tag'

**'Do It like A Dude'** may have thrust Jessie into the spotlight, but the success of the second single 'Price Tag' far surpassed it. The uptempo, 'feel-good' track was co-written by Jessie, Dr. Luke, Claude Kelly and American rapper B.o.B, who also features on the record. The song is about Jessie trying to 'make the world dance' by forgetting all about money. Nick Levine of Digital Spy said the song was 'a little bit corny' and compared it to the track that Jessie wrote for Miley Cyrus: the 2009 cheesy hit 'Party In The U.S.A.'. Despite the bop factor, Levine admitted there was no denying Jessie's 'spunky likability'.

## Million Seller

The track reached No. 23 in the US, but it topped the charts in 10 countries, including the UK, Ireland and New Zealand, and reached the Top 10 in 19 countries. As of early 2012, the single was the fourth-best selling in the UK and had sold 1 million copies. 'Price Tag' is also one of the most watched music videos of all time, having reached over 200 million total views by April 2012. Jessie even released a special Christmas version, while UK grime artist Devlin features on the UK version. The video features an oversized teddy bear, a money tree and Jessie as a ballerina in a large jewellery box.

*'It's not about the money...*
*We don't need your money...*
*We just wanna make the*
*world dance; forget about*
*the price tag.'*
*Jessie J lyrics*

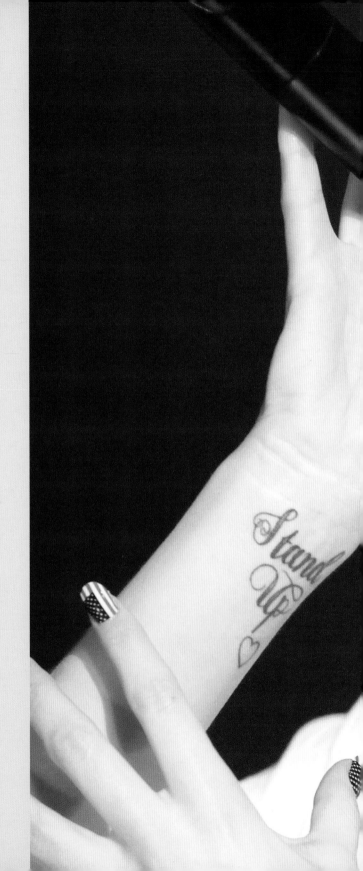

'She is a *gifted writer* besides being an *unbelievable singer*. She has been performing on stage since she was a *child*, so she *knows* what she wants. She knew certain people she *really wanted* to work with and didn't want to do *one session* after another, *writing* with a *different person* every day. She wanted to *focus* on a *small number* of *creative* people.'

Jason Flom

## Predicted Star

'Price Tag' saw the singer's profile continue its dramatic ascent, and being awarded 'tweeting' praise from the likes of Kylie Minogue and Paloma Faith only served to further inflame the mounting hype surrounding Jessie's debut

Music magazine *Q* awarded her Best Video for 'Do It Like A Dude' in 2011, and she was also nominated for Best Breakthrough Artist and Best Female Artist. She picked up Best Female Artist at the 2011 Urban Music Awards, where the single 'Nobody's Perfect', as well as her album, also received nods of approval. The year 2012 saw her up for three BRITs – Best British Female Solo Artist, Best Breakthrough Artist and Best Single ('Price Tag') – but she lost out to Adele, Ed Sheeran and One Direction, respectively. Her double-platinum smash hit 'Price Tag' won her an MTV Video Play award in 2012.

*'You've gotta have fun as well, write it down, take pictures, make sure it's a journey, the journey is way more important than where you end up.'* Jessie J

## Sing Out, Sister

Reviews of *Who You Are* were mixed. *NME* gave the album five out of a possible 10, praising her 'undeniably potent' voice and early commercial success, whilst noting evidence of a perceived 'identity crisis', which the reviewer thought understandable after writing hits for so many others. The review also criticized the

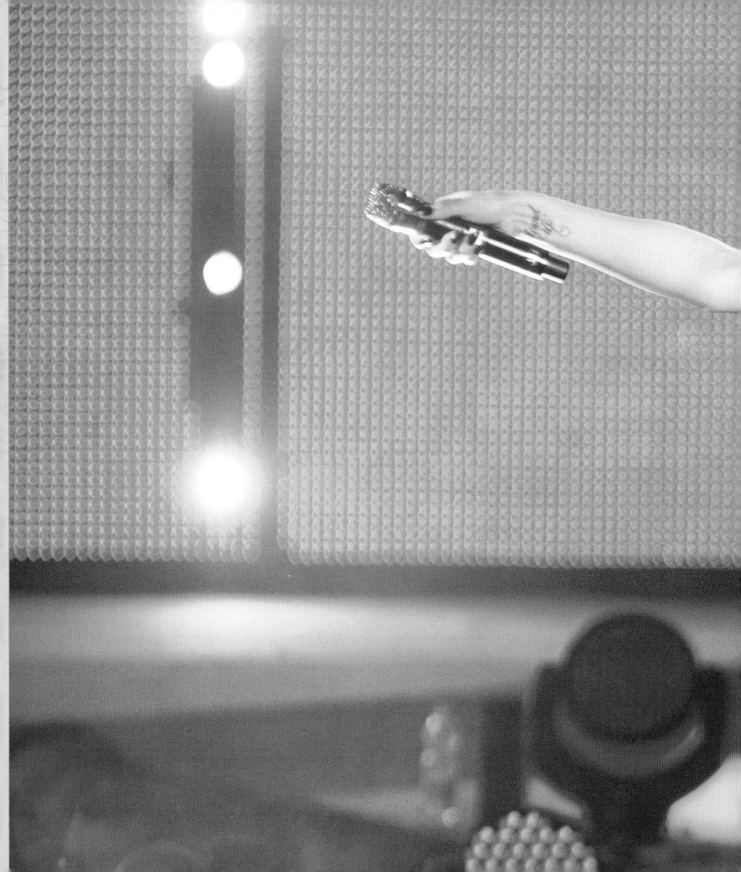

## Out Loud!

**The year following** the release of *Who You Are* would be a whirlwind of interviews, television appearances, industry events, festivals, concerts and tour dates for Jessie. She undertook two headlining tours (Stand Up and The Heartbeat Tour) and was a guest and/or performer on a number of television shows, including *The Graham Norton Show*, *Alan Carr: Chatty Man*, *NBC News Today*, *The Ellen DeGeneres Show*, *Late Show with David Letterman* and *The Late Late Show*. She made a splash in France, where she performed for the country's version of *The X-Factor*, as well as an open-air gig at the Cannes Film Festival. She also began picking up magazine covers, such as *Q*, *Shout* and *Glamour*.

## The Show Must Go On

Jessie's schedule was set to have been even more hectic, until injury rudely interrupted it. The singer was supposed to be opening for Katy Perry's California Dreams Tour but an injury sustained on 12 June 2011 during rehearsals for the Capital Radio Summertime Ball disrupted these plans. She ruptured several tendons in her foot, but she did not initially let the injury stop her and went on to perform her Capital set the next day from a gilded throne. On 25 June, she played the legendary Glastonbury Festival from the throne again, telling the crowd that she was defying doctor's orders. And fair enough, it was Glasto after all – a dream gig for any artist.

'I have the opportunity to fly the flag in such places as America, Australia, Japan. It's just overwhelming. It feels like there is a movement right now and I am so honoured to be one of the artists to be a part of it.'

Jessie J

Five days after Glastonbury, Jessie had surgery on her injured foot. It was announced that she was pulling out of festivals T in the Park, T4 on the Beach, Orange RockCorps in Wembley, iTunes Festival, Lovebox and Oxygen. She returned to the concert circuit in late August, playing sets at V Festival and The Big Chill. She was later the 'house artist' at the 2011 MTV Video Music Awards, where she performed from the throne again, but this time wearing a cast.

*'Keep making nervous jokes with the doctor and he keeps looking at me blankly. Which is making me laugh even more. It's getting serious. I just took my nose stud out.'*

*Jessie J, tweeting before knee surgery*

## Stand Up, Heartbeats

Jessie's first headlining tour Stand Up was a mere warm-up for the singer. It featured seven dates across the UK, and kicked off in Glasgow on 31 March 2011, taking in Bristol, Birmingham, Manchester, London and Dublin before finishing up in Belfast at the Mandela Hall on 9 April.

The Heartbeat Tour announced on Capital FM on 1 June was the big one, kicking off in the UK in October 2011. The original 11 UK dates were expanded to 14 due to high demand. Jessie lined up UK grime artist Devlin, who features on the UK remix of 'Price Tag', as supporting act. Finishing in the UK in early November, she played a single show at the F1 Music Rocks Festival in São Paulo, Brazil, later that month, before taking time out to promote herself in the US.

## Down Under

Resuming touring in March 2012, she played five Australian gigs, although she had to cancel a further three dates (two in Australia and one in New Zealand) due to voice problems. She later tweeted: 'Feel so good apart from sounding like Marge from The Simpsons. I wanna give my vocal cords a hug', along with a picture of her using a steam machine to help her get better. The reception she got from Aussie audiences – on the other side of the Earth – helped Jessie realize just how famous she had become. 'To be able to play shows here to 8,000 or 9,000 people a night and everyone knows the words to every song; not even singles – just makes you feel so humbled and so grateful,' she said before jetting off for a gig each in Singapore, Malaysia and Indonesia. 'Singapore is such an amazing city,' Jessie tweeted on 19 March. 'It's absolutely beautiful … the lights, the atmosphere.' She also added, 'I want to match my show tomorrow with the way this city makes me feel … *magical* :).'

'I have to spray myself with lots of Britney Spears' Fantasy perfume before I go on. If I don't I can't perform to my best. Everyone thinks it's hilarious. I keep having to buy more.'

Jessie J, revealing her bizarre tour ritual

> 'I know it is a big thing to say but I am ready for it. Whether it happens or not I believe I can push boundaries. As long as I am happy ... I can't make any mistakes really.'
>
> Jessie J

## Ol' USA

**Jessie, like countless artists before her**, was to find breaking America a challenge. Speaking in June 2011, Jason Flom, head of Lava, said that the plan was always to focus on the UK initially. 'It made sense to have the UK take the lead on this project because she lives there and things can happen so quickly over there,' he told a music journalist. 'In the UK, BBC Radio 1 is dominant nationally and their support gives you a lot of recognition overnight, whereas in the US you have to go one station at a time, and build in many different ways. England is also a much smaller country but still has influence in the US – the tastemakers over there have an impact on what happens over here.'

## A Small Splash

Jessie's album hadn't been a complete failure; she appeared on *Saturday Night Live* in March and 'Price Tag' performed relatively well, reaching No. 23, while her album made it to No. 11 on the *Billboard* 200 chart.

Jason Flom also added, 'This is not a sprint, it's a marathon – we see her as an important artist in the long-term. I think the US is going to be a huge market for her. We had a top 10 debut in the US, and this is a rare feat for a new artist.' Sure enough, thanks to single 'Domino', Jessie's popularity and fame stateside have skyrocketed. The Dr. Luke-produced

track did not feature on *Who You Are* originally, but it appeared on a November re-release, along with two other new tracks. The video was launched on Boxing Day in the US, where it appeared at No. 2 on the *Billboard* Dance Chart and No. 6 on the *Billboard* Top 100.

## 'Domino'

Jessie performed the track on the US *X Factor* in November 2011. Wearing a colourful wig and outfit, the singer was accused in some quarters of being a duplicate of Katy Perry, both in image and sound. 'Domino' is undoubtedly reminiscent of 'Last Friday Night' – as illustrated by some good mashups posted on YouTube – and Dr Luke was behind both hits. Following her performance, Simon Cowell, Paula Abdul and Nicole Scherzinger gave Jessie a standing ovation, whereas the fourth judge, LA Reid, remained seated, unsmiling. Rumour has it that he was still bitter after Jessie rejected his attempts to sign her years earlier.

## Pop Crush

Jessie J loves a range of music and artists, and has collaborated with acts including David Guetta (on track 'Laserlight') and James Morrison (on 'Up'). Her *X Factor* USA performance saw her on the bill the same night as Will Smith's daughter, Willow Smith. Both artists have expressed interest in future collaboration. Pixie Lott, Katy Perry and Wretch 32

'It felt great, my Twitter went mad! I've got about two million people now trying to find out who I am. They're like "why does Justin Bieber like Jessie J?"'

Jessie J, commenting on Justin Bieber praising her talent on Twitter

have all spoken of a desire to work with Jessie, who has admitted that her biggest pop crush is still Rihanna. Jessie has named plenty of other candidates, including Lil Wayne – whose 'swagger' she adores – and Nicky Minaj. 'There are so many people I want to work with; Prince, Beyoncé, Eminem, Drake. I am going to wait to see what happens, see how the world takes my album.' Jessie's music has also featured on film soundtracks; 'Who You Are' was used in the third instalment of the American 3-D street dance *Step Up* franchise, and the track 'Sexy Silk', used by Nivea, had previously made it onto the film soundtrack of the 2010 comedy *Easy A*.

'I am proud to say that I am British and I am proud to say that I am ready to take on the likes of Pink, Beyoncé and Katy Perry and really make a name for British icons.'

Jessie J, speaking to Metro in 2011

'I've never denied it, even four or five years ago when people used to talk to me about it, I always said I've always liked *girls* and I've always liked *boys*. I've never put my *sexuality* in a *box* and I've never *named* it, and I've never *labelled* it.'

*Jessie J*

# Look At Me

**Jessie's futuristic**, heavily made-up street style reflects the singer's confidence as well as her urban tunes. The girl is well maintained. She has come a long way since the days when she used to 'live in a Gap jumper, tracksuit bottoms and a fake flower in my hair' – a look she now describes as 'shocking'. However, to some at least, her outlandish, provocative outfits mean she is still firmly cemented in the 'shocking' category. Jessie is one of the few who can pull off a body stocking with ease. Her penchant for skin-tight clothing bagged her the No. 16 spot in *FHM*'s 2012 Sexiest Women of the Year poll, where she was described as a 'Catsuited Songbird'.

# Mixing It Up

She shows no fear when it comes to fashion, teaming bright patterns with tough-chick black leather, oversized accessories and heavy make-up. It is difficult to distinguish which labels she is wearing – she likes to mix in vintage and high street with, say, Vivienne Westwood and Chanel. Occasionally, she pulls out all the old-school elegance stops, such as for the *Glamour* Women of the Year Awards in 2011, where she wore the sparkly floor-length black Dolce & Gabbana gown, and she even swept back her trademark fringe. 'Style, to me,' she has proclaimed, 'should be what makes you feel comfortable.' Fair play to the lass, who feels comfy wearing a nude body stocking with black 'tattoos' on live television, as she did for a 2011 appearance on *The Graham Norton Show*.

## All About The 'Do

Perhaps the most striking part of Jessie's look is her hair. Even though she is actually a natural blonde, she has become known for her inky black, poker-straight bob and severe, straight fringe. The *Pulp Fiction* overtones go well with her ghetto-pop image. People have stopped her many times in the street to ask if her hair is really a wig. 'I say, "Yeah yeah, you can buy it down Hamley's."' Jessie has experimented with a few different styles. 'I did hair modelling for four years. I had green and blue hair, a mohawk, but I always kept coming back to this bob. It's like my comfort blanket.' Her bob has been purple, she has worn black curls, blue streaks and rock chick waves; in spring 2012, *The Voice* saw her with on-trend, colour-dipped extensions. In 2011, she announced she would be shaving her head for charity the following year. 'It's hair. It will grow back. Even if it takes 2 years, if it saves lives it's worth it. Even if it's 1 life that's something,' she said via Twitter.

'It was *never* like, I need a *gimmick*. I need a *look*. I've always had the *hair*, *lipstick*, long *nails*.' *Jessie J*

# Something Personal

Jessie made headlines in July 2011 when she confirmed rumours about her sexuality. It was revealed that the star likes both men and women, and has had at least one relationship with a female. She stated in an interview on the *In Demand* radio show on 3 March 2011, 'I've never denied it. Whoopie doo guys, yes, I've dated girls and I've dated boys – get over it.' She told *Glamour* magazine, 'It's important to me to be open and honest about [my bisexuality]. My Mum and Dad have known for years and were super cool, my sisters made jokes about it because they were married with kids and I was the rebellious one. I had a girlfriend and tattoos. Because I haven't tried to hide it, people have gone, "Oh, she's so cool about it, so we're cool about it."' At the time of writing, however, gossip magazines were full of speculation about her 'secret boyfriend' and some even suggested the mystery man was fellow Brit musician Tinie Tempah.

'Style should not have a brand. I don't think that style's about how much money you wear on your back, or your shoes ... I just think it needs to be an artistic, creative outlook on who you want to look like.'

Jessie J

'I never wanted to be called a hypocrite, but I didn't want my sexuality to become a gimmick. There are lots of people who go, '"Oh I'm bisexual." No. You've kissed your friend.' Jessie J

'I'm just proud I can be a decent influence on girls. As long as I'm known for my music first and all the other stuff comes second, I'm cool with that.'

Jessie J

## Look Up To Me

**Despite her wild outfits**, Jessie is often looked upon as a good role model for the younger generation, which is a responsibility that the singer takes seriously and enjoys. In a promotional video for glacéau vitaminwater™, filmed in September 2011, Jessie spoke of the shock of the previous six months, which had seen her fame rise meteorically. 'My life has changed drastically, from nobody knowing who I am to being a household name. I go on YouTube and I see little kids dressing up as me,' she says in the video, promoting her sideline gig as official Olympic Ambassador for the drinks brand. She goes on to describe herself as 'excited' at the prospect of inspiring and influencing youngsters in a positive way.

## Top Role Model

The role model label was further cemented when she topped Capital FM's list of 'top role models in pop' – voted for by the fans. According to the radio station, it was Jessie's honest lyrics and positive attitude that won her the title. 'Her songs tell you how life actually is and teach you what to expect out of it,' one Jessie J supporter said. 'She lives life the way she wants to and doesn't let anyone stand in her way,' added another. Jessie beat Lady Gaga, JLS, Beyoncé and Justin Bieber to the top spot.

'As a mum of 3 girls I feel the lyrics and meaning in her songs encourage them to be true to who they are and that there is more to life than money and materialistic things. We love nothing better than blasting out her tunes and singing at the top of our voices.'

Jessie J fan, posting on official forum

## No Stick Insect

Unlike many young people in the spotlight, Jessie is yet to bow to any real or imagined pressure to be stick thin. As a size 8, the singer is certainly fit and very slim for her height, but she has said she thinks it important 'to be healthy in any situation'. Comments she made at the end of 2011 about her New Year's resolution to gain weight certainly went against the grain and grabbed headlines. She says, 'It's important to

> *'It is important to embrace the limelight, and I know it sounds like a cliché but the kids need me not to let them down. I feel like the role model thing has chosen me.'*
>
> Jessie J

know when you need to gain weight or when you need to lose weight and be healthy.' She said she thought a bit of extra bulk would help her withstand a tough touring and performance schedule set down for 2012. 'I think I'm too skinny,' she told *More!* in March, whilst confessing to MTV, 'I was front of the queue for legs, back for boobs and bum.'

## Clean Living

Jessie J claims to have never ever been drunk. 'I'd never get paralytic because I couldn't handle it and I wouldn't want to be someone else's responsibility,' the star has said. She has admitted to getting slightly tipsy on the very odd occasion, but insists that 'alcohol is not my confidence'. The singer does not smoke or take drugs either – a stance that stems from the minor stroke she suffered as a teen. She knows she needs to take care of her body so it will take care of her. 'Having bad health has made me realize I can't take anything for granted and I must look after my body. I'm a clean living girl.'

The singer has publicly wondered whether her teetotal stance – and therefore the lack of incriminating, scandalous photographs of her falling out of nightclubs – led to the media's fascination with her sexuality. 'It's the only thing they [media] can grab onto – they're like, "She never drinks and she comes out of the party looking like she did when she went in, damn her!"' The singer has vowed she will never do drugs and says, 'Singing is my drug.'

# My Heartbeats

**Jessie's devotion to her ever-expanding fanbase** appears stronger than that of many of her contemporaries. She credits her success to the overwhelming support she has received. Following in the footsteps of the likes of Lady Gaga and her 'Little Monsters', Jessie was quick to give her followers a shared identity: 'I call them my heartbeats because without them I wouldn't exist,' she has said.

'My fans are ... mental. They are the most incredible fanbase that I have ever seen come together so quickly.'

Jessie J

'It was a very strong deal, especially in today's climate, but I felt like I might never find another artist as gifted as Jessie J.'

Jason Flom, president, Lava Records

# Tech Savvy

The remarkable pace at which Jessie's fanbase has grown is largely due to her superb publicity skills and, in particular, to her use of social media. She has all the usual accounts: Myspace, Facebook, YouTube and, of course, Twitter. The singer is a regular tweeter and she passed

the 3 million-follower mark in March 2012 – built up from 1.3 million followers five months prior. By May 2012, her official Facebook artist page had amassed over 6 million 'Likes'.

One of the new generation of performers who have grown up with the internet and social networks, right from the start of her career Jessie has demonstrated a true affinity with the medium and how to use it to engage with her audience.

## Dare Jessie

*Dare Jessie* is Jessie's very own online television series in which she takes on various challenges – usually embarrassing ones – set by fans. Early fans keen to set her tasks were fellow famous faces, including Justin Timberlake and celebrity blogger Perez Hilton: 'Which is cool, of course it is, but I want everyone to get involved,' Jessie said at the time. The girl sure knows how to flatter her fanbase, but she always appears 100 per cent genuine. 'Just because someone's famous don't make them more important,' she insists. The clips, which can be viewed via a Myspace portal specifically designed for her, are the perfect example of how Jessie has used social media to engage with her existing fans, whilst helping to create armies of new ones. The first episode, which was released in 2010, also featured a behind-the-scenes look at the filming of her first ever music video ('Do It Like A Dude'), as well as the goings-on of her first ever photoshoot.

'I call [fans] heartbeats. Heartbeats keep you alive, and I wouldn't be here as a musician without my fans.'

Jessie J

## Totally Devoted

She opens the first clip with: 'The Jessie J journey is just getting started, and I wanted to do this show *Dare Jessie* so you guys can watch me every single step of the way and come with me on my journey.' She goes on to say she wants her fans to be able to get to know her behind the scenes, as well as in front of the camera. Her first dare was set by her 'good friend' Tulisa's band (at the time): N-Dubz. They dared her to go to Trafalgar Square dressed in a gorilla suit and 'do a gig'. The results are fairly hilarious – or 'stupidly embarrassing but loads of fun', according to Jessie. 'I really don't want to do this but I'm doing it for you, for the entertainment, so you'd better appreciate it,' she jokingly commented while wagging her oversized gorilla finger at the camera.

'I love how you don't take a single minute for granted; you are living my dream. One day I hope to be just like you.'

Fan named nackie enthuses on jessiejonline.com

# The Voice

**In October 2011**, Jessie J was confirmed as one of four coaches for the newest talent show on the block, *The Voice UK*. 'This is the first talent show that focuses on what really matters when you're a singer. It's all about the voice,' Jessie said at the time. Presented by Holly Willoughby and Reggie Yates, Jessie was a hit right from the start, holding her own on the panel of swivelling chairs, despite being up against Black Eyed Peas superstar will.i.am, Danny O'Donoghue and the legendary Tom Jones. The stars recorded a cover of The Black Eyed Peas' 'I Gotta Feeling' and the buzz surrounding the new show was huge; as a result, *Britain's Got Talent*'s ratings slipped, as the two shows went head-to-head.

'It's important to dream big – you've got to try it to see if it can happen. That's what I love about this industry: that it's possible to take an idea and see if it can come true.'

Jessie J

# Looking Forward!

The show's adverts described the mentors as 'four of the world's biggest music superstars'. Jones said of Jessie's performance on the show: 'She's a strong character. She is young and she knows what she wants.' Jessie told *More!* in March 2012 that a future collaboration with Jones was on the cards to happen 'very soon'. She also said filming was incredibly emotional. 'I can relate to these artists. I've been in their position and I know just how scary it can be.' Jessie has proved more than able to hold her own against her more experienced co-judges. She has developed a reputation as a feisty chick, yet often shows a softer side, having been moved to tears on several occasions by the talent.

Around the time when the first *The Voice* auditions were under way, in January 2012, Jessie revealed that she had started recording her second album. She was also looking forward to playing her 'Heartbeat' set at some of the UK's most popular festivals, including T in the Park, Wireless and the Isle of Wight Festival.

# Still Getting Started!

With her credibility and experience as a songwriter, along with a seemingly endless supply of street cred, positive energy and motivation, the Jessie J journey seems to be only just beginning. She is so articulate, down to earth, focused and glamorous that it is easy to forget the star is still in her early twenties. However,

she has revealed that her new album will be different: 'There will be a lot more pain in the lyrics … now that I'm happier, I won't be afraid to explore my pain. But in a good way,' Jessie told the *Daily Star*. She then added, 'I want to explore every aspect of music more on the next album, from different styles to my voice to what I sing about to who I get to duet with.'

## Three Words

When asked to 'sum herself up' in three words, she told *Glamour* magazine: 'Honest, emotional, happy.' Whatever projects or directions Jessie takes in the future, she will clearly chosen her own path. She told *More!* that she wanted people to see how hard she works. 'Every day I wake up and think of ways I can be a better singer. Most of all I want to be remembered for my voice.'

'I base my confidence on purity and I want to be a role model … I want people to know that I am an unedited version of myself. I plan to expose the good and the bad to show that life is about being Who You Are.' Jessie J

# Further Information

## Jessie J Info

**Birth Name**    Jessica Ellen Cornish

**Birth Date**    27 March 1988

**Birth Place**    Chadwell Heath, Essex

**Height**    1.75 m (5 ft 9 in)

**Nationality**    British

**Hair Colour**    Naturally dark blonde; variety of other styles (see far right)

**Eye Colour**    Green

## Discography

### Albums

*Who You Are* (2011)

## Singles

**2010:**    'Do It Like A Dude' (UK No. 2)

**2011:**    'Price Tag' (UK No. 1)

        'Nobody's Perfect' (UK No. 9)

        'Who's Laughing Now'

        'Domino' (UK No. 1)

        'Who You Are' (UK No. 8)

**2012:**    'LaserLight' (UK No. 5)

## Tours

Stand Up Tour    (2011)

Heartbeat Tour    (2011/12)

## Awards

### BBC

**2010:**    BBC Sound of 2011

### BRIT Awards

**2011:**    Critics' Choice

### BT Digital Music Awards

**2011:**    Best Newcomer

        Best Female Artist

        Best Song 'Price Tag'

### Capital FM Awards

**2011:**    Best Role Model In Pop

## MOBO Awards

**2011:**    Best Newcomer

Best UK Act

Best Album *Who You Are*

Best Song 'Do It Like A Dude'

## MTV Video Play Awards

**2012:**    2× Platinum 'Price Tag'

## Q Awards

**2011:**    'Do It Like a Dude'

## Urban Music Awards

**2011:**    Best Female Artist

## Virgin Media Awards

**2011:**    Best Newcomer

## Top Ten Jessie Dos

## Glamour Awards

**2011:**    Woman of Tomorrow

## Harper's Bazaar Women Of the Year Awards

**2011:**    Breakthrough of the Year

# Online

**jessiejofficial.com**

Official site in many languages, with forum, blog, news and store

**myspace.com/jessiejofficial**

Check this site out for Jessie's latest songs, videos and Dare Jessie

**facebook.com/JessieJOfficial**

Check out Jessie's latest writing on the wall

**twitter.com/jessiej**

Join the millions of other followers to see what Jessie has to say @JessieJ

# Biographies

## Alice Hudson (Author)

From New Zealand, Alice fused twin passions for writing and music while a student, reviewing and interviewing international bands and DJs. She is currently based in London, writing and researching for corporate clients across a wide range of sectors, from health and fitness and financial services, to social media and entertainment. Other titles for Flame Tree include *Katy Perry: Rebel Dreamer*, *Will & Kate: Fairy Tale Romance* and *Adele: Songbird*.

## Mango Saul (Foreword)

Mango Saul has been a music, lifestyle and entertainment journalist for ten years. Some of his highlights include having breakfast at Waffle House with rapper Ludacris in Atlanta, sharing a bed with Destiny's Child for a *Smash Hits* cover interview and being sent an ice-cream costume for no reason. As editor of Sugarscape.com, Mango has seen the site grow to over 4 million page views per month and was shortlisted for Digital Editorial Individual 2011 at the AOP Awards.

# Picture Credits